SAWYER | BERSON

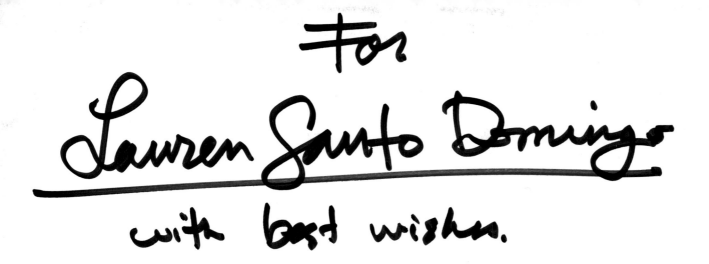

For
Lauren Santo Domingo
with best wishes.

SAWYER | BERSON

HOUSES AND LANDSCAPES

BRIAN SAWYER & JOHN BERSON
WITH MAYER RUS

Brian Sawyer

12/23

RIZZOLI
NEW YORK

New York · Paris · London · Milan

CONTENTS

PREFACE BY
BRIAN SAWYER & JOHN BERSON

WE ESTABLISHED Sawyer | Berson in the summer of 1999 with the goal of creating a multidisciplinary firm where we could devote ourselves to a wide variety of projects, primarily the design of houses and gardens, a selection of which is presented in this book. Our curiosity has led us to explore the vast history of design and the boundless range of traditional and modern styles, with each project providing an opportunity to learn something new. Along the way, we have tried to avoid trends and fashion in pursuit of the more enduring qualities of appropriateness, quality, and beauty.

Our methodology and approach were cultivated during our years at the office of Robert A.M. Stern, where we worked together in the 1990s. At the time, Stern's burgeoning practice was still relatively small, which afforded us the opportunity to work on a diverse array of projects with distinct design vocabularies, ranging in scale from residential to institutional to large-scale commercial developments. The workload was often overwhelming, but there was always great energy and enthusiasm, fueled by constant critical and creative discourse.

Early in our practice, we had the good fortune of working across a variety of genres, including a mid-century modern house and a shingle-style estate, both on the ocean in Long Island, New York; a roof terrace of steel, concrete, and glass in Manhattan; and an expansive sculpture park for a museum in New Orleans. These early projects enabled us to establish the process we've implemented for the ensuing two decades: a disciplined synthesis of the client's needs and tastes with the pragmatic requirements of site and form to create a unified composition in a singular style.

We develop site plans and house designs in tandem, as the two are inextricably linked formally, functionally, and aesthetically. A successful site and landscape design balances spatial, experiential, and ecological imperatives in a way that appears natural and inevitable. The process of designing a house unfolds in much the same way. Channeling the unique spirit of a particular client, we plan and tailor our homes to accommodate the overlapping functions of use and flow that typify modern living. This is common to our work regardless of style.

Every conversation about style starts with the client. Our responsibility is to listen carefully and identify precisely what resonates with them. For inspiration, we not only rely on our architectural memory and knowledge but continually refer to our favorite moments in history as well as a core group of influential designers spanning many centuries and styles. As inveterate explorers, we always seek precedents that stretch our imagination.

The guiding principle of Sawyer | Berson has remained unchanged since the founding of our practice. We see every assignment as an opportunity to create unique designs that mine the past, embrace the present, and anticipate the future. We take pride in the diversity of our portfolio, knowing that no two projects are alike; the houses and landscapes we create are as delightfully individual as the people who inhabit them.

INTRODUCTION BY
MAYER RUS

MY FIRST ENCOUNTER with Sawyer|Berson's work involved a typical exercise in Manhattan high-rise voyeurism. Roughly two decades ago, as I was looking out on the city from my seventeenth-floor apartment, I noticed a construction site for a lavish rooftop terrace—replete with a modernist dining pergola, alfresco lounge, outdoor shower, and a series of expansive architectural planters—perched atop the building across the street. This seductive urban Eden, perfectly framed in the proscenium of my window, held my fascination for months, especially as the lavish plantings of Japanese white pine, bayberry, hydrangea, and lavender began to mature and blossom. Set within a taut architectural framework, the romantic eruption of greenery, simultaneously contained and untamed, was, in a word, enchanting. I struggled in vain to identify the designers of this idyllic wonder, and at one point, after spying a party unfolding on the terrace, I even attempted to blend anonymously into the crowd entering the building.

I failed to infiltrate the party after the greeter at the door discovered my ruse and summarily sent me packing. But a few short weeks later, I fortuitously crossed paths for the first time with architectural designer and landscape architect Brian Sawyer and his partner, architect John Berson. Mystery solved. I eventually wrote an article about the terrace for *House & Garden*, my employer at the time, and I have been chronicling the work of their firm, Sawyer | Berson, ever since. But even as the scale and ambition of their projects have continued to expand and flourish,

the essential animating forces of the partners' enterprise have remained constant: their facility in brokering a nuanced rapprochement between classical and modern design idioms; their grounding in the principles of landscape architecture; and their insistence on suitability and apposite forms derived from the specific demands of site, context, and client.

Born and bred in New York City, Berson honed his craft at Princeton and then at the Harvard Graduate School of Design. Sawyer, an Indiana native, studied music and biology at Wabash College before obtaining his master's degree in landscape architecture from the University of Virginia. The two met in the early 1990s in the office of Robert A.M. Stern Architects, a crucible of design exploration and a training ground for many of today's preeminent architects and designers. In 1999, Sawyer and Berson struck out on their own, christening their newly formed partnership with the design of their mid-century modern project in Bridgehampton, a house that draws inspiration from Richard Neutra and Rudolph Schindler, with subtle nods to Frank Lloyd Wright.

Sawyer | Berson's broad inheritance from Stern is apparent in the firm's research-driven approach, its openness to a wide range of vernacular styles, and the intensely collaborative spirit of the office. Rather than an enforced division of labor, Sawyer and Berson contribute equally to the work at hand, refining each other's ideas and impulses in the search for proper architectural form. The partners perceive the logical continuity between traditional and contemporary design, recognizing in each a set of prompts that can be employed toward the same end: harmonizing the desires of the client with the possibilities of the site in an ideal way. Their many hyphenate revival designs are not slavish reproductions but rather translations or interpretations of norms and ideas into a modern ethos. The partners pay homage to historical antecedents by demonstrating their enduring beauty, appeal, and adaptability to the rhythms and rituals of contemporary life.

Sawyer and Berson possess the easy erudition of those who have studied long enough and well enough to allude with confidence rather than quote with cockiness. They understand the concept of modern as a lens rather than a style. Indeed, Thomas Chippendale, from whom Sawyer | Berson derived the pattern on the railing that surmounts the roof of the firm's Colonial Revival house in Southampton, described his designs in 1754 as modern, based as they were on French models in the *goûte moderne*. No less an eminence than Le Corbusier reiterate d a similar idea: "To be modern is not a fashion, but a state," Corbu averred. "It is necessary to understand history, and he who understands history knows how to find continuity between that which was, that which is, and that which will be." Unlike the tourist who learns, say, conversational Italian, Sawyer and Berson understand the grammar, syntax, vocabulary, and the history embedded in the architectural phrases their houses articulate so eloquently. Their traditional designs are not

revivals in the sense of an empty corpse but reanimations brimming with generative potential.

A similar kind of time warp emerges in the firm's distinctly modern homes—such as their Southampton contemporary and modern projects—which they imbue with the classical virtues espoused for centuries by the likes of Vitruvius and Palladio. These long, lean structures, assiduously distilled into compositions of orderly rectilinear planes, achieve a palpable sense of generosity and comfort from the precision of their conception and execution. Sawyer and Berson are perceptive historians who grasp the essential endurance of proper scale, proportion, material, form, and light in architecture, which renders distinctions between traditional and modern inapt, clunky, and even old-fashioned. In the words of the pioneering minimalist Donald Judd, "You can't exaggerate the importance of proportion. It is almost the definition of art and architecture."

Sawyer | Berson's dexterity navigating the seemingly contradictory languages of design perhaps derives from their understanding of time from the *longue durée* of landscape architecture, time as geological rather than chronological, in which context the gulf between the eighteenth century and the twenty-first is just a drop in the bucket. From this perspective, historical time is compressed, revealing a fundamental similarity of design imperatives. Sawyer | Berson's Colonial, Greek, and Georgian Revival buildings are structurally taut, with strong lines and clear planes, just like their contemporary designs.

All are based on the same exigencies, both philosophical and morphological, conveyed by basic geometric forms regardless of their level of ornamentation.

The Colonial Revival project in Southampton again provides an apt example of Sawyer | Berson's method, the traditional morphology of the house's exterior contrasting with the client's desire for a more modern feel inside. The simplified interior program of walls stripped of moldings and furniture that emphasizes clean lines over ornament is distinctly modern, but it also speaks to early New England pragmatic sensibilities, sans the austerity, underscoring the pure in Puritan. One might also consider the partners' strategy of removing old master paintings from their aureate frames, instead setting them flatly against solid brass sheets or smooth velvet-covered planes, as they did in their room at the Kips Bay Show House and their booth for a fine art dealer at the TEFAF art and antiques fair the same year. Unframed, the paintings acquire a muscley vitality, as if freed from years of baggage and confident in their unfaded beauty and relevance.

Sawyer | Berson's approach is always fixed on negotiating the unique demands of place and client. Their practice is marked by a cultivated sensitivity to context—visual, topographical, and historical. In their hands, architecture is an exercise in nurturing the essence and essentials of a particular place in the most appropriate way possible. The animating spirit of architecture—home, family, hearth, genius loci—remains unchanged,

even as the forms of expression differ. These expressions can be aesthetic and decorative, but more than that, they are tethered to an intuitive understanding of the traditions that gave rise to them, the sympathies they were designed to evoke, the anxieties they were meant to soothe. Those fundamentally human needs—sleep, food, love, laughter—are unchanging. Sawyer | Berson comprehends the meaning of home as sanctuary, both restful and sacred, inspired and inspiring, a hallowed place mediating between the self and the greater beyond.

The firm's grounding in and love for landscape architecture cannot be overstated. Musing on the form and siting of Greek temples, the great classicist Edith Hamilton wrote: "To the Greek architect the setting of his temple was all-important. He planned it seeing it in clear outline against sea or sky, determining its size by its situation on plain or hilltop or the wide plateau of an acropolis. He did not think of it in and for itself, as just the building he was making; he conceived of it in relation to the hills and the seas and the arch of the sky." Regardless of the scope of their commissions—whether it be architecture, landscape, interiors, or some combination of these artificially discrete practices—Sawyer | Berson's work proceeds from an acknowledgment of the mutually ennobling relationship between buildings and nature.

This acknowledgment bears fruit most obviously in the seaside villas captured so dramatically in the photography for this book. But it also pertains to the firm's work on the mean streets of New York City. The massing of shapes and plantings on the urban terraces crafted by Sawyer | Berson plays volumetrically off the rise and fall of the skyline around them, just as a Greek temple complex would respond to the topographical features surrounding its site. Once again, context is key. In their Manhattan townhouse project—and even in Sawyer's own Victorian-era apartment that has neither gardens nor terraces—the interior architecture and design respond not only to the architectural envelope but also to the human need for connection to light, air, and the sustenance of the natural world.

The gardens they create, much like their houses, represent a locus amoenus, an idyllic and often idealized natural environment (like Eden or Elysium) where people frolic among trees and flowers and the better parts of human nature shine in pastoral splendor. Pastoral poems—from the ancient writings of Hesiod and Theocritus to the Romantic effusions of Christopher Marlowe and Percy Shelley—often feature echoes, putting a person in literal conversation with nature, their thoughts turned to commentary when rejiggered by forces out of their control. In all their projects, Sawyer | Berson reckons with a horizon that seems limitless, an inescapable reminder of the smallness of man against the geogenic scale of nature that can be enervating or invigorating depending on one's ego. The partners' solution is to frame the landscape, the endless horizon of the sea or the urban skyline becoming performers on a stage enclosed by a proscenium of carefully executed hard- and softscape interventions. Nature can be engaged

but not controlled, enjoyed like any performance, its denouement unknown.

Sawyer | Berson's ability to hold seemingly opposing forces in amicable tension—landscape and architecture, interior and exterior, traditional and modern—is the backbone of the firm's praxis, as is their commitment to privileging suitability over fashion. Mies van der Rohe, who promulgated a vision of modernism based on a philosophical and moral imperative, opined that "Architecture is the will of an epoch translated into space." Sawyer and Berson categorically reject Mies's doctrinaire attitude and its presumption of an overriding will that negates the pluralism of contemporary society. They subjugate the very notion of style to the crucial substance of context and client desire. Many architects and designers who want to be taken seriously as modernists have little feeling for antique pleasures, but there is a generous, catholic embrace of many different kinds of beauty in Sawyer | Berson's work. Their marker resides in subtlety, agility, and an unerring sense of what is apropos, and their work will endure precisely because it gathers strength and beauty from those qualities proven over centuries, indeed millennia, to be profoundly, self-evidently enduring.

SOUTHAMPTON MODERN

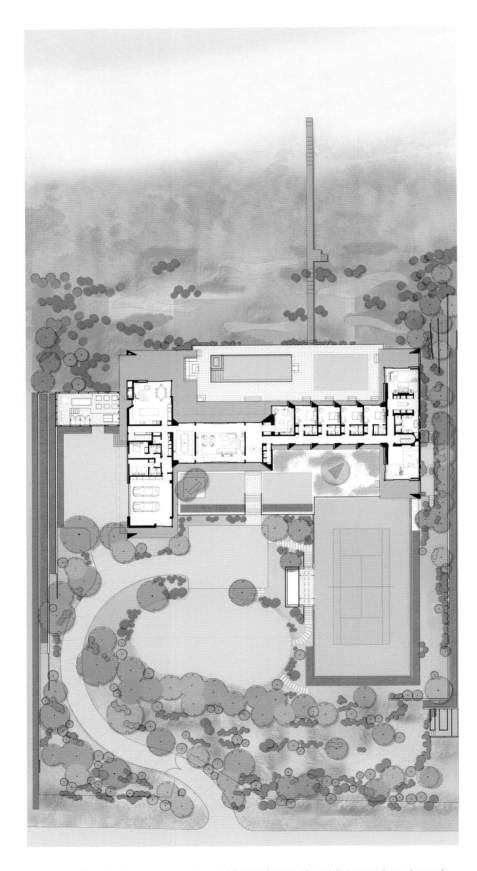

PAGES 12-13: The bedroom wing, viewed from the north, with its wedge-shaped walls and soffits of stained and wire-brushed sapele. Native bayberry shrubs and a steel sculpture by Mark di Suvero seem to float in the gravel-and-grass courtyard garden. ABOVE: Plan of the main floor and site.

The entrance to the house is up a broad flight of cast-stone steps, couched between plantings of bayberry, juniper, and grasses, which leads to the entry hall and ocean terrace beyond.

THE CLIENTS WERE looking for new summer house, one that would comfortably accommodate their family of five and be suitable for both intimate gatherings and large parties. We were inspired by the Long Island beach houses designed by architects Horace Gifford and Arthur Erickson in the 1960s and 1970s, characterized by their rigorous geometries and highly selective materials palettes.

The imposing waterfront site had magnificent views of the Atlantic Ocean to the south and Shinnecock Bay to the north, so it was important that the house be sufficiently elevated to take advantage of those sweeping vistas. At the same time, the clients desired a home that would have a low profile, barely visible from the street. In response, we designed the house as a single-story structure, linear and low in its massing, set at the perfect elevation by raising the site more

than twelve feet. The house is largely one room deep to provide unimpeded views both north and south from the major spaces.

The interior architecture was a wonderful collaboration with Stephen Sills, the clients' interior designer. Stephen was instrumental in uniting the clients' vision with our own, assuring that the interiors and the exterior would speak variations of the same language.

The landscape design for the 4.5-acre site included an extensive restoration of the dunes, which had been eroded over time. Through careful grading and planting we were able to conceal the house from the neighbors and the road, and at the same time create discreet outdoor spaces including a tennis court, lawns, and various gardens. The result is a landscape design that melds the imperatives of ecological responsibility with the clients' specific needs and wishes.

PAGES 16-17: A view east along the northern flank of the house with Shinnecock Bay beyond. The terrace of grass and crushed stone is planted with thunderhead pine and bayberry. In the foreground is a steel sculpture by Mark Di Suvero. ABOVE: Hand-finished plaster partitions define the enfilade leading from the dining room to the living room. OPPOSITE: The entry hall opens onto the pool terrace with the restored dunes and ocean beyond. PAGES 20-21: The sliding glass walls of the living room open north to Shinnecock Bay and south to the Atlantic Ocean. The metal and soapstone fireplace rests below the hand-finished plaster chimney breast.

PAGES 22-23: A view from the breakfast room through the dining terrace to the dunes and ocean. PAGES 24-25: The oceanfront façade viewed from the dune boardwalk. The intersecting single-story volumes of the house echo the contours of the dune landscape. ABOVE: The cast-stone diving platform with the restored dune and boardwalk beyond. OPPOSITE: The bedroom hallway leading to the primary suite and gym, with white oak floors and paneling. PAGES 28-29: A sunset view of the house from the northeast.

EAST END COMPOUND

OUR CLIENTS had just purchased a twelve-acre oceanfront estate in Long Island's East End, and were looking for an architect and landscape architect to make some changes to the existing main house and site. What ensued was a wonderful collaboration that entailed a complete transformation of the property.

The reconceived main house was designed as a center-hall Colonial Revival reminiscent of an East End shingled farmhouse but on a larger scale. The five-bay central volume is flanked by a pair of double chimneys that conceal a whale-watch deck. To either side are gable-roofed wings, modulating the large scale and conveying the impression of a historic house that had been added to over time. The entry façade is deliberately understated, with double-hung windows and a simple entry porch. The south waterfront façade is characterized by expansive glazing and

a broad second-floor screened porch with majestic views over the dunes to the ocean beyond.

The guest house was designed as a traditional shingle-clad Long Island farmhouse in sympathy with the eighteenth-century barn nearby, which was carefully restored. Our decoration scheme was intentionally modest to convey the level of comfort and casualness expected of a summer house.

The existing site was mostly lawn on the north side, bereft of trees and plantings, with a driveway down the center slicing the property in two. It was redesigned with a tree-lined elliptical drive surrounding a large central lawn, creating a multilayered view north from the main house to balance the expansive ocean view to the south. An extensive scheme of plantings, gardens, and outdoor living areas, implemented over a period of twenty years, is now maturing.

PAGES 30-31: The ocean-facing south façade of the house as seen from the beach path. The four chimneys of the main block conceal a whale-watching deck with spectacular views in all directions. PAGE 32: The view looking south to the main house over the grand elliptical lawn is framed by London plane trees with an underplanting of shrubs and perennials. PAGE 33: The shaded drive leading to the guest house is planted with dogwood, locust, and cherry trees with a variety of perennial underplantings. PAGES 34-35: A view from the shaded drive at sunset to the main lawn over sweeping perennial borders is framed by London plane and styrax trees. PAGES 36-37: The front of the main house with its entry porch facing north provides the perfect spot to watch the sun set over the lawn or enjoy a summer storm under cover. ABOVE: The open-air pool pavilion echoes the vernacular architecture of the structures within the compound. OPPOSITE: A detail view of the west wing of the house with its gable and gently sweeping roof line.

ABOVE: Astilbes and veronica blooming beneath the plane trees and stewartias bordering the driveway.
OPPOSITE: Semicircular bluestone steps flanked by evergreens and flowering shrubs lead to the guest house's front door and its surround inspired by an early-eighteenth-century Long Island farmhouse.

ABOVE: The stair hall's mahogany railing was copied from a captain's house in Sag Harbor. The floors are bleached reclaimed heart pine. OPPOSITE: A view from the kitchen to the living room with its eclectic furnishings and objects. PAGES 44-45: The living room features a collection of old waterway maps, dozens of vintage books, and antique furnishings acquired on the North Fork of Long Island.

PAGES 46-47 The kitchen cabinetry is painted a pastel sky blue with countertops of Petit Granit limestone. Above are shelves displaying a collection of nineteenth-century glassware and ceramics. ABOVE: The Green Bedroom features ink drawings by Hugo Guinness. OPPOSITE: In the bunkroom are a mid-nineteenth-century mahogany American chest of drawers and wallpaper featuring native wildlife.

PAGES 50-51: A view through the south guest house porch with the barn beyond.
OPPOSITE: The barn, one of the few original buildings from the eighteenth-century farms
that once occupied the area, seen here from the guest house lawn. It was carefully
stabilized and restored and is now used for events and recreation. ABOVE: An interior
view of the old post-and-beam barn with its hand-hewn oak trusses and pine floor.

WAINSCOTT BEACH HOUSE

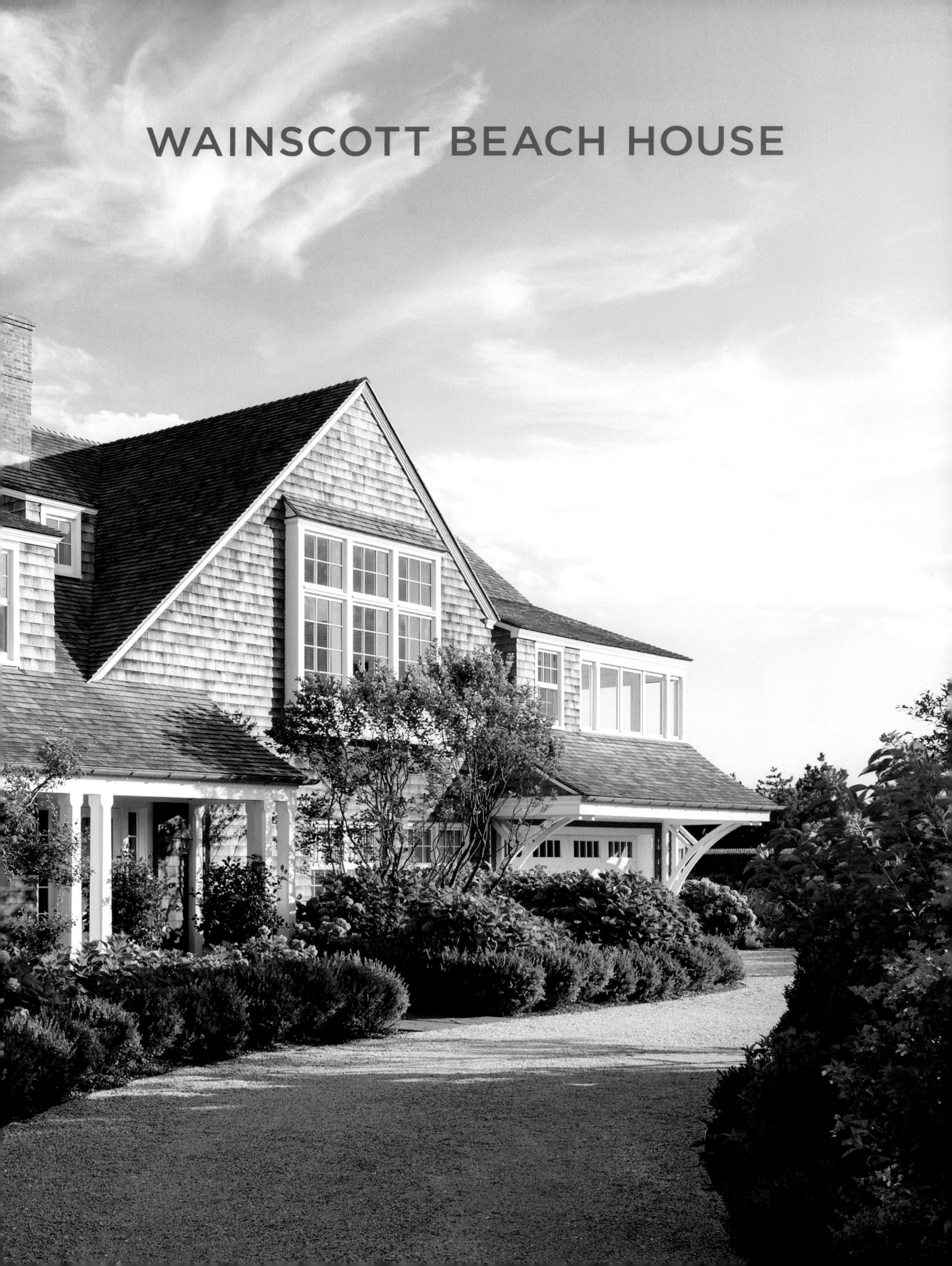

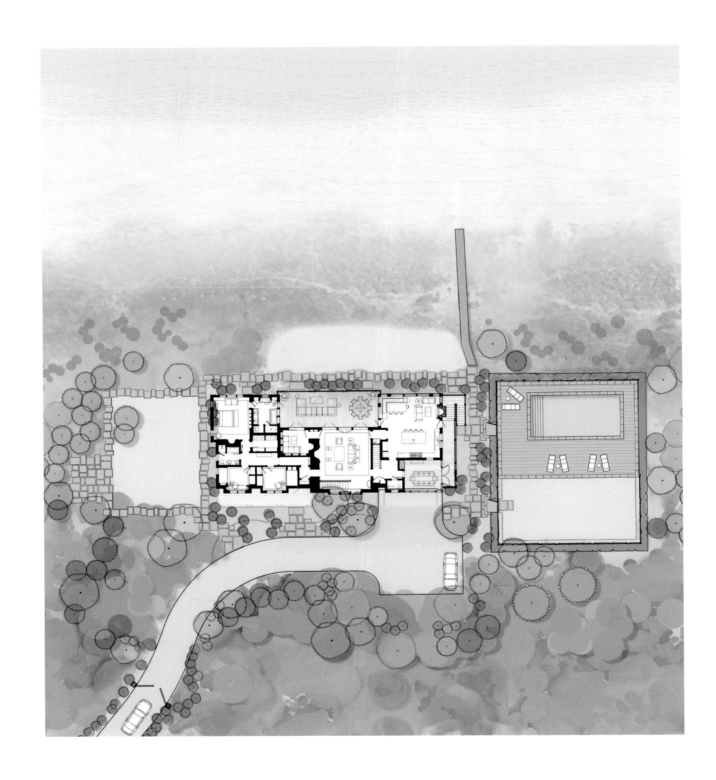

PAGES 54-55: The entry façade viewed from the northeast, with its sweeping roofs, crisp detailing, and antique brick chimneys. The oriel window in the central gable floods the living room with light from the north. ABOVE: Plan of the second floor and site. OPPOSITE: On the west side of the house, the second-floor dining porch and kitchen overlook the pool.

OUR CLIENT came to us to for a project on the beautiful shoreline of Wainscott, New York, to replace her existing house, which was set precariously on the dune and no longer met her needs. In response, a new house was designed to maintain the spirit of the old house and satisfy the new program. The client wanted to avoid the typical gambrel-roofed Hamptons-style house, so for inspiration we turned to the austere houses of John Calvin Stevens in Maine as well as the modest houses crafted by Alfred Scheffer in Amagansett.

Consideration had to be given to maintaining the dramatic ocean views that, on the first floor, would be obstructed by the dunes. The result was an "upside-down" house, with the living room, kitchen, and family bedrooms situated on the upper level, and the guest bedrooms and media room on the lower. The exterior is clad in red cedar shingles and characterized by simple gables and shed dormers, articulated with minimum moldings and trim, with large arching brackets supporting deep overhangs.

For the site design, we fashioned a sequestered landscape, featuring a swimming pool and outdoor recreation areas concealed by robust native plantings that also provide screening and channel views from the rooms on the lower level.

ABOVE: The entry hall features a fireplace and hearth of antique brick, with a reclaimed floor of old-growth pine.
OPPOSITE: The oriel window on the north side of the living room above the entry stair.

A view of the ocean from the living room.

ABOVE: Just off the living room is the intimate den with bookcases of white oak. OPPOSITE: The kitchen features floors of old-growth pine, white-painted cabinetry with antiqued glass, and a beadboard ceiling. The Dutch door leads out to the pool.

The ground floor family and TV room with a painted wood beam and beadboard ceiling.

ABOVE: The mahogany and Carrara marble vanity looks out to the ocean. OPPOSITE: A ground floor guest room with double-hung windows and a door to the garden and dune beyond.

OPPOSITE: At the base of the kitchen stair is a pantry and flower room with varnished mahogany countertops. ABOVE: The mudroom hallway has a Petit Granit limestone floor and louvered closet doors. PAGES 70-71: A view of the house from the northwest with its sweeping roof and deep overhangs. PAGES 72-73: Nestled behind the dune is the pool deck, shielded from the ocean winds by the clipped privet hedge.

MID-CENTURY MODERN

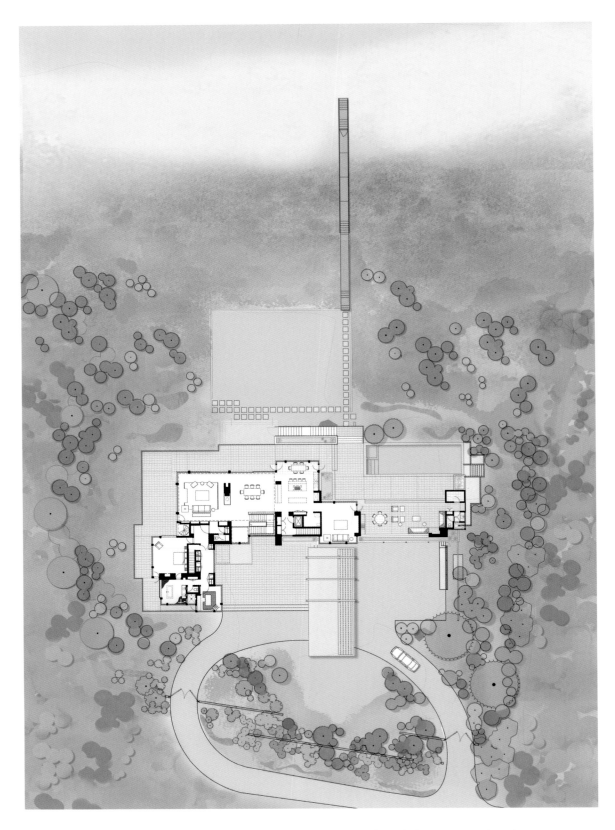

PAGES 74-75: The north profile of the house, with its interlocking roofs and chimneys, against the ocean backdrop. ABOVE: The plan of the main floor and site. OPPOSITE: The entry stair hall on the ground floor features pigmented poured concrete floors and walls of Douglas fir and Utah limestone. The stair's concrete treads are supported by blackened-steel beams. The mahogany sliding doors were inspired by Rudolph Schindler's Kings Road house. PAGES 78-79: The north side of the house, with its Utah limestone piers and chimneys and mahogany-clad walls. The carport with its deep cantilevers was a specific request of the client.

AN INCREDIBLE opportunity came our way cour-
tesy of the late interior designer John Barman,
who had kindly introduced us to the clients after he
saw the Colonial Revival house we had renovated
on Hook Pond in East Hampton. The clients wanted
a mid-century modern house, and we shared their
passion for this era's architecture and design.

This truly remarkable oceanfront site in
Bridgehampton, New York, not only had sweeping views of the Atlantic Ocean to the south but
also overlooked beautiful wetlands and Sagg
Pond to the northeast. To address these views,
the house was elevated, with the principal rooms,

along with the swimming pool and pergola
terrace, on the upper floor, and the children's and
guest bedrooms on the lower level.

For style and massing, we took our lead from
the clients and studied the houses of Richard
Neutra and Rudolph Schindler. These led to the
open plan, with interlocking volumes and deep
cantilevers of the roofs and terraces, as well as
the use of materials and details authentic to the
period. These include Utah limestone and mahogany cladding on the exterior, and concrete floors,
natural wood millwork, and reproduction period
fixtures and hardware on the interior.

ABOVE: The primary-suite dressing area with the study beyond. The floor is stained cork tile, the millwork and doors are stained Douglas fir, and the ceiling lights are reproductions of the originals found in Richard Neutra's Kaufmann House in Palm Springs, California. OPPOSITE: The living room has wide expanses of glass looking south to the ocean and east to Sagg Pond with a clerestory sitting above the deeply cantilevered roof of the deck beyond. The room is separated from the dining area by a three-sided fireplace of Utah limestone. PAGES 82-83: The house facing the ocean in bright morning light. PAGES 84-85: The main ocean terrace on the second floor, with its cantilevered roof and mahogany soffit, appears to float above the concrete deck. The anodized aluminum railing was inspired by a house in Spain.

COLONIAL REVIVAL

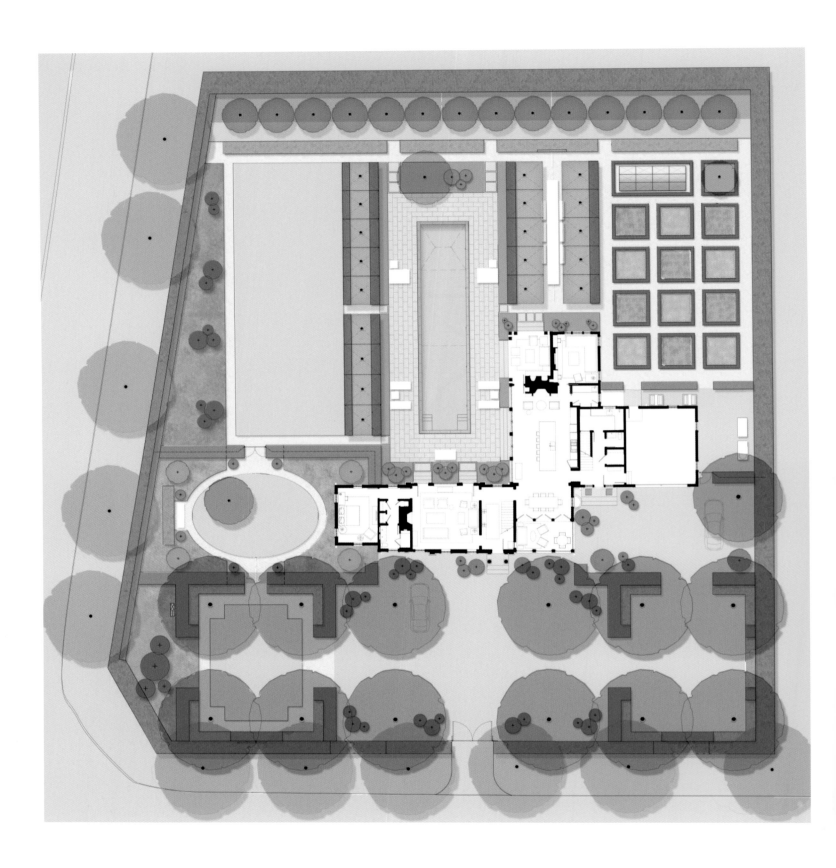

PAGES 86-87: A view of the façade from the street framed with clipped privet and London plane trees. The central pediment is supported by two-story Doric pilasters and flanked by a Jeffersonian balustrade. ABOVE: The plan of the main floor and site. OPPOSITE: The west garden parterre features statue-like Emerald Green Arborvitae underplanted with vinca and surrounded by clipped privet hedges and crushed oyster shell pathways.

AFTER SEEING an image of our very first project on Hook Pond in East Hampton, our clients came to us for a new house in the heart of the village of Southampton, New York. They wanted the house to fit in gracefully with the surrounding historic architecture, and it seemed to us that an authentic interpretation of the local Colonial Revival style was the appropriate choice for this project.

The character of the house arises from an unexpected juxtaposition of the exterior and interior styles. The exterior features classical detailing, including the central pediment and columned portico, with pilasters framing the front and poolside porches. It is clad in white-painted cedar shingles and crowned with a decorative Jeffersonian balustrade. In contrast to the formality of the exterior, we took a modern approach to the interior architecture. We selected a simple palette of lime-painted plaster walls void of baseboards or crown moldings, and light-stained white oak floors and framed openings. The bathrooms are limestone with tadelakt plaster walls.

For the interior decoration, we were inspired by the spare northern European style, with the selected furnishings and artwork emphasizing materiality. For the gardens, the clients were clear about their desire for a rational, geometric layout. The design incorporates a motor court of crushed oyster shells and a grid of London plane trees, interspersed with clipped American boxwood. An elliptical garden serves as a transition to the rear landscape, comprised of manicured boxwood parterres, large perennial borders, a dining allée of pleached linden trees and a swimming pool surrounded by a cast-stone terrace.

ABOVE: A London plane tree set into the crushed oyster shell border. OPPOSITE: The entry stair hall looks onto the pool terrace and is finished with walls of grey-tinted lime paint and floors of white oak. PAGES 92-93: The living room features a blackened-steel fireplace and chimney breast with a photograph by Jack Pierson. Linen-slipcovered upholstery is grouped with a hemp rug and steel-and-wood occasional pieces. PAGES 94-95: On the living room wall is a photograph by Chip Hooper. The flanking openings to the entry hall have white oak jambs.

ABOVE: A row of littleleaf linden trees planted in an oyster shell border lined with clipped yew and boxwood hedges. OPPOSITE: The kitchen walls are finished with a slate-grey lime paint, the floors are white oak, and the island counter is white glass. French oak armchairs and a steel drum table sit on a vintage Moroccan rug.

ABOVE: A guest bedroom features a white lacquered four-poster bed, lime-painted walls, sheer linen curtains, and a selection of photographs from the Robin Rice Gallery. OPPOSITE: A guest bathroom with sand-colored tadelakt plaster walls has a floor of Spanish limestone. PAGES 100-101: The house's garden façades overlook the swimming pool terrace, which is framed by clipped boxwood, yews, and linden trees.

ABOVE: The teak dining table for thirty-six guests sits on a bed of crushed oyster shells and is flanked by rows of littleleaf linden trees. OPPOSITE: A view of the garage wing, with its windvane-topped cupola, across the north parterre garden. The clipped boxwood borders are inset with alternating plantings of barberry shrubs and grasses. PAGES 104-105: The swimming pool's coping is flush with the surrounding cast-stone deck. At the far end is a stand of cryptomeria, providing a backdrop for a red Japanese maple.

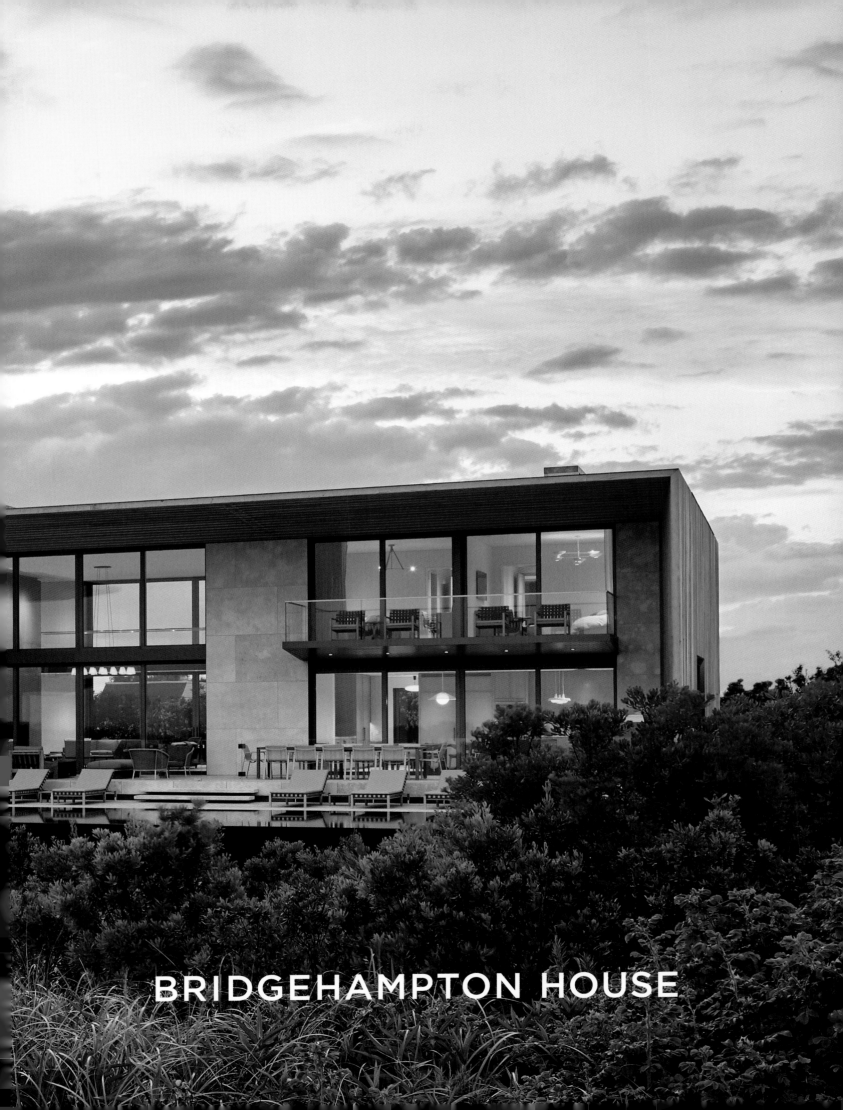

BRIDGEHAMPTON HOUSE

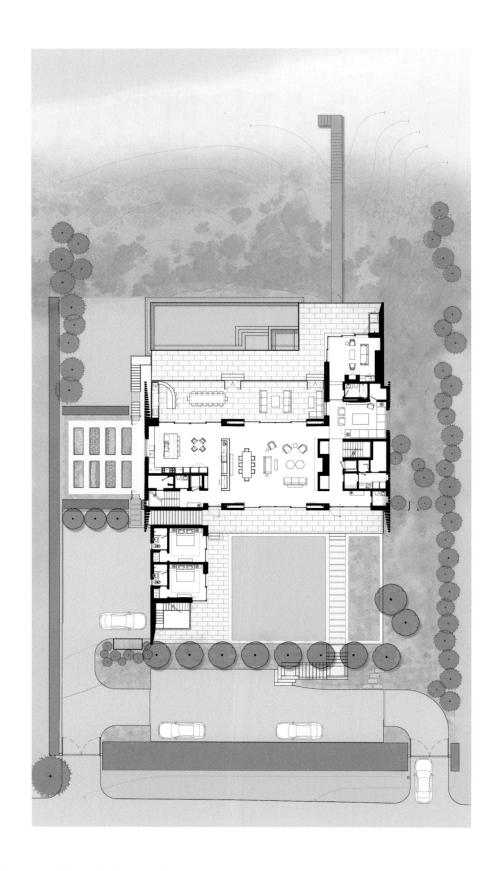

PAGES 106-107: The ocean side of the house, with its interlocking masses and double-height living room at its center, viewed at sunset from the dune. ABOVE: The plan of the main floor and site. OPPOSITE: The entrance to the house, with a walkway, steps, and walls of Jerusalem limestone. The two-story canopy is Alaskan yellow cedar, and the doors, windows, and balconies are dark-bronze aluminum. PAGES 110-111: The guest wing is set perpendicular to the main body of the house, slipping under its canopy to modulate the mass and rooflines.

THE CLIENTS had enjoyed their house on this stunning oceanfront property in Bridgehampton, New York, for decades, but they were seeking to replace it as the home no longer suited their needs. Having admired a house we designed nearby, they came to us for a new and unique contemporary beach house that would serve as a multigenerational summer home.

This house features two distinct bedroom wings connected by a double-height living room that also unites the principal living rooms on the main level with the swimming pool terrace and its outdoor kitchen, which face the ocean. On the second floor, the two wings are linked by a balcony spanning the living room.

This area of Bridgehampton has been a laboratory for an eclectic array of modern architects since the 1960s, including Charles Gwathmey and Norman Jaffe. We were inspired by this tradition to create a house with a particular vision and style, and the result is a structure with a clear hierarchy of geometric forms, rendered with a limited palette of Alaskan yellow cedar, Jerusalem limestone, and bronze-colored aluminum windows, doors, and balconies.

To meet environmental guidelines, the house was placed on an elevated plinth, which provides a front lawn and garden for the main entrance to the north and the pool terrace to the south. The dune was stabilized and restored with native plantings and is traversed by a wood boardwalk. Vegetable and cutting gardens, as well as play areas, are nestled in the protected areas flanking the house. The beautiful interiors were done by our friend and colleague Damon Liss.

PAGES 112-113: Anchoring the double-height living room is a paneled wall of quarter-sawn walnut together with a fireplace surround of Eros Grey marble. The bridge walkway connecting the two wings can be seen at the upper right.

ABOVE: The stairway, handrail, and screen are bleached white oak. OPPOSITE: Along the dining area is a double-height wall paneled with quarter-sawn walnut. The floor is sandblasted and brushed Jerusalem limestone. PAGES 116-117: The kitchen and breakfast room has stained walnut cabinets, and the countertops and backsplash are grey quartzite.

PAGES 118-119: The primary bedroom, with its wraparound terrace, opens at its corner to expansive views of the ocean. ABOVE: The primary bathroom tub and niche are sheathed in silver travertine and washed in natural light from the skylight above. OPPOSITE: The west wing bordering the pool terrace reaches out toward the ocean with wedge-shaped roof overhangs and cantilevered balconies. PAGES 122-123: On the ocean side of the house, the double-height canopy shields the dining terrace adjacent to the pool deck. The dune landscape is reflected in the horizon-edge pool.

The house was designed to convey the impression that the center mass, with its gable roof and white-painted brick and granite schist walls, was the original Federal style home, and that the flanking cedar-shingled wings were later additions. The gravel driveway encircles one of the 150-year-old Siberian elms. PAGE 126: The driveway meanders through the front lawn, encircling one of the majestic Siberian elms. The clipped hedge conceals the sunken tennis court. The oak and maple trees were planted to line the driveway and provide a backdrop to the west. PAGE 127: The plan of the ground floor and site. The sunken tennis court is at the bottom right, and Georgica Pond is at the upper left.

GEORGICA POND HOUSE

LOCATED IN East Hampton, New York, this beautiful waterfront property had a charming gambrel-roofed cottage that had fallen into disrepair, as well as several mature Siberian elms. We were asked to create a new home for a young family incorporating the original structure and preserving these magnificent trees.

We conceived the new house with a central pavilion flanked by two wings, one of which incorporates the existing cottage to take advantage of its proximity to the pond. The central pavilion was designed not only to accommodate the main living spaces but also to serve as the visual anchor. To lend it mass and substance, it was clad with whitewashed brick and granite schist. The intent was to create a narrative in which the new central pavilion is perceived as the original house while the cedar-shingled wings appear to be later additions. The Georgian Revival style of the "original" house was chosen as a complement to the classic style of the cottage.

The extensive program included a central living room, kitchen and dining room, swimming pool and recreation room, playrooms, studies, and a gym, as well as bedrooms for family, guests, and staff. We collaborated on the architecture with our friend and colleague Steven Gambrel, who executed the beautiful interior design and decor.

The landscape plan included a sunken artificial-grass tennis court surrounded by low brick walls and hedges. We focused the views and relationship to the pond by careful clearing and manipulation of the understory, as well as selective pruning of the existing pines. Complex and subtle grading was required to create a gently contoured landscape that would integrate and enhance the site's natural features.

ABOVE: The entry porch to the guest wing. OPPOSITE: A view east through the vaulted breezeway, with a beadboard ceiling and bluestone paving, which sits between the main house and pool house wing. Beyond are the hydrangea borders and clipped privet hedge surrounding the tennis court.

ABOVE: An angled stair, with wood paneling and simple attenuated conical balusters, ascends to the primary bedroom suite and abuts the white-painted brick and granite schist wall of the living room to the right. OPPOSITE: The entry hall at the center of the house, with its high ceiling, transomed cased openings, and antique Dalle de Bourgogne limestone floor, lends a rustic feeling to this formal link between the wings of the house.

OPPOSITE: The living room, with a high shiplapped wood ceiling and subdued moldings and trim, has a massive limestone fireplace designed by Steven Gambrel. The tall French doors open onto a lawn facing the pond.
ABOVE: The kitchen accommodates informal dining, opens out onto a screen porch, and overlooks the swimming pool.

ABOVE: The porch entry off the mudroom. OPPOSITE: The north porch off the guest bedrooms overlooks Georgica Pond. It features a beamed wood ceiling, simply detailed wood piers, and bluestone paving.

ABOVE: The layered landscape on the southern border of the property includes clipped hedges, manicured lawns, and mature pine and maple trees. OPPOSITE: A view from the lawn facing Georgica Pond.
PAGES 138-139: The sunken tennis court of artificial turf is concealed by a border of clipped hedges and a trellised fence. The steps lead up to the bluestone-paved viewing platform, and in the background is a stand of oak and maple trees that conceals the driveway beyond.

SOUTHAMPTON CONTEMPORARY

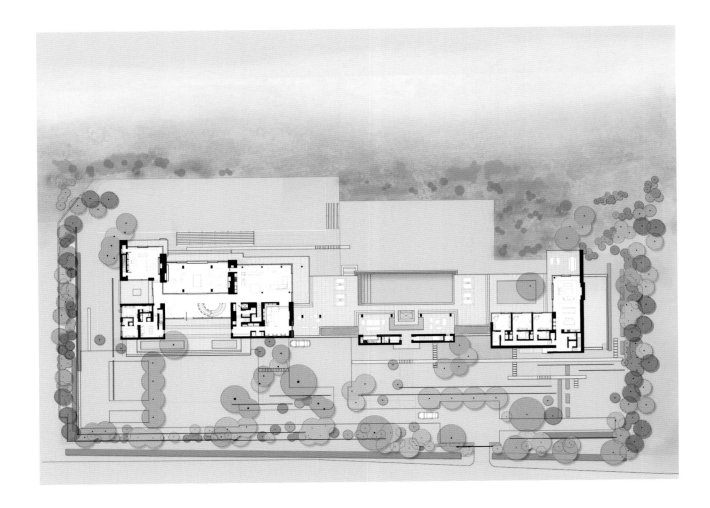

OUR CLIENTS, the interior designer Kelly Behun and her husband, came to us in 2002 after seeing a waterfront house we had designed in Bridgehampton, New York. They admired the home's transparency and lightness, and wanted to replicate these effects on their spectacular five-acre oceanfront site in Southampton Village. They envisioned a similarly transparent house, but with a brighter contemporary palette typical of Behun's style.

The site has unobstructed views south to the Atlantic Ocean and north to Coopers Neck Pond. The stringent setback requirements dictated a long and narrow structure parallel to the ocean, and we took this opportunity to create a string of three buildings, mostly one room deep, facing the water. The main house, swimming-pool cabana, and guest house share a materials palette of Luget limestone walls, Valders limestone decks, teak-

framed windows and sliding doors, and eaves of white enameled metal. The three buildings are linked by a common basement, which contains a cinema, recreation room, garages, and gym.

The main house is a two-story structure comprising an entry hall, loggia, living room, kitchen and family room, library, and upstairs bedrooms. Corner windows and large expanses of glass are precisely deployed to take advantage of the views. At the center of the pool cabana is a spa with a rooftop aperture and a view across the pool to the ocean beyond. The L-shaped guest house was designed with modernist Southern California precedents in mind.

The interior architecture, design, and decorating are by Kelly Behun in collaboration with Bonetti/Kozerski Architecture. The landscape was designed by Gary Hilderbrand and Eric Kramer of Reed Hilderbrand.

PAGES 140-141: Among the home's magnificent ocean vistas is this striking view from the pool cabana, looking out over the limestone spa deck and horizon-edge pool to the dunes and Atlantic Ocean. PAGE 142: The plan of the main floor and site. PAGE 143: The double-height entrance hall with a balcony walkway connecting the bedrooms. The painting is by Jean-Michel Basquiat. PAGES 144-145: This view from the dunes highlights the home's interlocking volumes and broad expanses of glass. The bright palette is primarily French Luget limestone, teak-clad doors and windows, and Valders paving. At the left, the swimming pool's wall is punctured by a window looking out to the dunes. ABOVE: The river-stone-lined reflecting pool at the east end of the house features a sculpture by Joel Shapiro. OPPOSITE: The library has eighteen-foot ceilings, full-height bookcases, and a desk and sofa designed by Kelly Behun.

PAGES 148-149: The ocean-facing kitchen and family room with features and furniture designed by Kelly Behun and Bonetti/ Kozerski. Bleached walnut, Carrara marble, and stainless steel are used throughout.
OPPOSITE: A view to the ocean from the family room. PAGES 152-153: The guest house, pool cabana, and swimming pool as seen from the main house's ocean terrace.

NORTH SEA MINIMAL

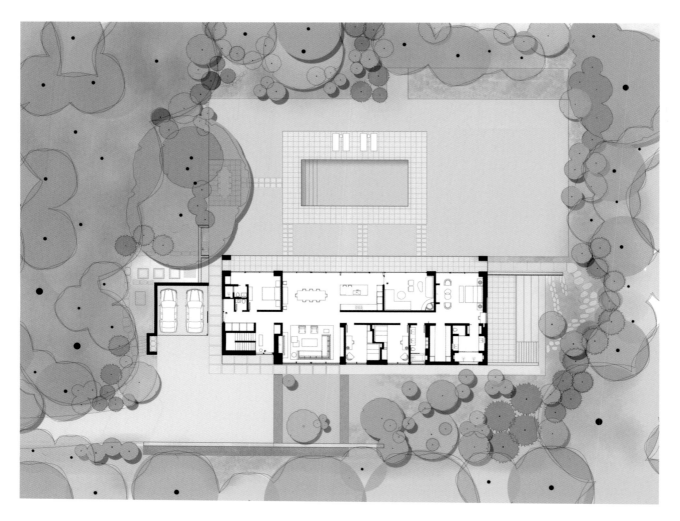

PAGES 154-155: The south side of the house with a portico spanning its full width. The walls are handmade brick, the doors and windows are anodized aluminum, and the roof is standing-seam zinc. ABOVE: The plan of the house and site. OPPOSITE: The primary bedroom viewed from the exterior. The handmade bricks are set with mortar made from imported porcelain sand. To the right is glimpse into the Moroccan-style loggia.

WE WERE THRILLED when our colleague and friend Richard Shemtov, of the furniture design and manufacturing company Dune, approached us about collaborating on a new house for his family in Southampton, New York. Our firm took on the planning and architecture of the home as well as the landscape design, and Richard designed and implemented the interiors, including the furniture and the fine millwork and cabinetry.

The project was truly an exercise in discipline. For the massing and detailing of the exterior, we sought to be as reductive as possible, assiduously avoiding superfluous detail that might distract from the purity of the composition. We created a one-story gable-roofed structure featuring a sheer transition from roof to wall, with no overhanging eaves or rakes. In the process of exploring a contemporary materials palette, Richard brought to us the beautiful handmade, cream-colored brick on the exterior, which provides the required architectural precision as well as an element of warmth.

The secluded, wooded setting required subtle clearing and careful grading to accommodate the house and its semi-concealed lower-level living spaces. The swimming pool was situated in the main lawn as a central feature of the landscape, seen from almost every room.

ABOVE: The front entry hall looking out to the motor court. The glass, wood, and bronze stair was designed by Shemtov.
OPPOSITE: The double-height volume of the living and dining room extends to the ridgeline of the house. Shemtov designed and fabricated the wire-brushed reclaimed wide-plank pine floors. PAGES 160-161: The dining area's doors lead to the pool and terrace beyond. PAGES 162-163: The beautiful kitchen designed by Shemtov features white oak cabinetry.

PAGES 164-165: The lower-level family and recreation room looking out to the tiered garden beyond. The seating area furnishings are by Dune. ABOVE: The primary bedroom features a full-height upholstered wall and has views of the pool and tiered garden below. OPPOSITE: An evening view of the house's full-length portico.

SAG HARBOR FEDERAL

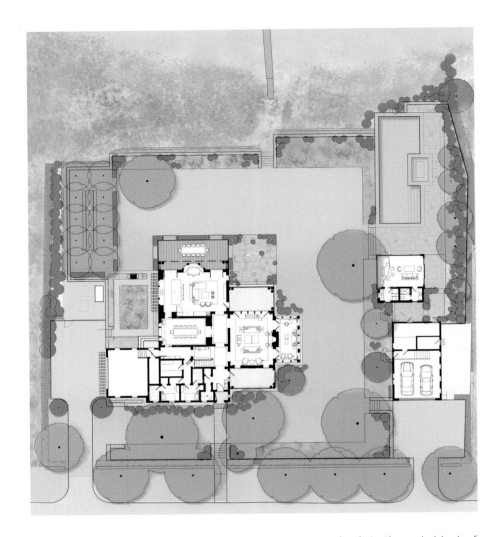

PAGES 168-169: The arrival up a flight of solid bluestone steps leads to the main block of the house with its Federal-style façade in white-painted clapboard with pilasters and denticulated entablature. ABOVE: The plan of the main floor and site. OPPOSITE: The living room porch abuts the house's white-painted shingled north block.

WE DESIGNED this house, set on a striking waterfront property in Sag Harbor, New York, for a couple with two young children and their friends and family. The site is set amid an array of historic houses on one of the village's most beautiful streets. The style of the house was inspired by the local architectural vernacular dating back 300 years to its settlement as a whaling center.

Specifically, we looked at the local Federal and Colonial architecture from the early eighteenth to mid-nineteenth centuries to derive inspiration for the architectural details that grace both the interior and exterior. The house is meant as a weekend retreat from the city, and

it includes generous outdoor living spaces along with the interior program. The handsome art-filled interiors were designed by our colleague Russell Groves.

The presence of wetlands presented a challenge for building on this sensitive site. Through a program of native plantings and soil remediation, along with carefully placed retaining walls, we were able to create a tiered landscape that incorporates views across a lawn and meadow towards the bay. Other landscape elements include a dining bosque, a walled kitchen garden, and perennial borders. A swimming pool and pavilion share sweeping views to the water.

ABOVE: The paneled dining room with a beamed ceiling provides an expansive backdrop for art. The picture window looks into the kitchen garden. OPPOSITE: The entry hall looking back through its front Dutch door has painted wood paneling, a cast plaster crown, and Petit Granit limestone floors. PAGES 174-175: The bay window breakfast niche in the kitchen and family room has a view south toward Upper Sag Harbor Cove. The floors are European oak.

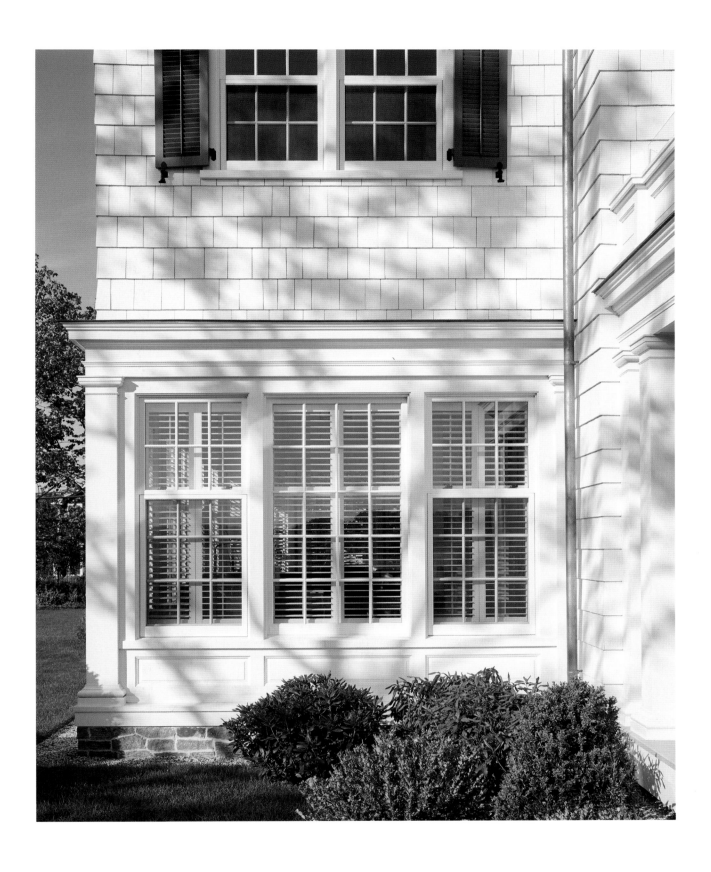

OPPOSITE: The view through the living room toward the study. ABOVE: The study wing beneath the house's shingled north façade is meant to appear as a glazed-in porch and rests on a rubble-stone foundation. PAGES 178-179: A deep planting border along the southern bulkhead, featuring grasses and perennials with contrasting foliage and flowers, provides a foreground to the bay view throughout the year.

ABOVE: The view to The Little Narrows across the cove from the dock. Along the shoreline, a bulkhead was removed to make way for wetland restoration and the reintroduction of indigenous plant life. OPPOSITE An allée of crape myrtle trees facing the water shelters a table for thirty guests for an alfresco meal.

NOYACK REGENCY

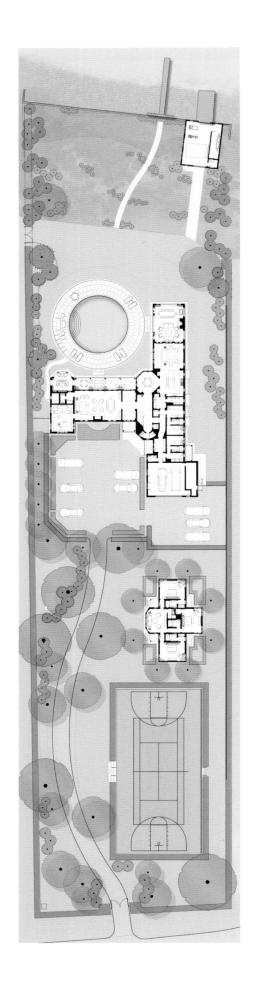

THIS PROJECT is situated on a long and slender two-acre waterfront site overlooking the coves of Sag Harbor, New York. The unique property had a wonderful old boathouse and dock that provided our client and his family access to the beautiful local bays.

The clients divide their time between California and New York City. For their summer home they preferred a more modern stucco house to a traditional shingled one, so we suggested the Hollywood Regency style. Two precedents came to mind: the 1930s Coral Casino Club in Santa Barbara and a deco-style house by John Staub in Houston. These precedents were a source for many features of this home, including the long terraces with their slender posts, the expansive loggia with its outdoor living areas, and the oversize French doors and casement windows. The octagonal central tower recalls the light-house-like gestures of the Coral Casino.

For the interiors, the streamlined decorative moldings defer to the architectural brio of the house's signature rooms and features: the sweeping main stair, the grand living room with its clerestories and monumental fireplace, and a double-height primary bath in the octagonal tower. The finishes and furnishings were done by architect and designer Daniel Romualdez.

For the landscape design, the gently curved driveway leads past the tennis court and guest house, both set in expansive lawns with perimeter trees planted for privacy. A wetlands buffer of native plantings lines the waterfront and bulkhead. A circular swimming pool, inspired by one in Beverly Hills, is the center of this home's summer lifestyle.

PAGES 182-183: The entry side of the house with its octagonal two-story volume enclosing the stair hall. The walls are cream-colored stucco, the windows are painted aluminum-clad wood, and the roof is cedar shingles. LEFT: The site plan. OPPOSITE: The entry porch has a standing-seam lead-coated copper roof. Through the front door is a view of the swimming pool and cove beyond.

ABOVE: The entry hall has an oak plank floor stenciled with a geometric trompe l'oeil pattern. The front door, with chamfered rectangular panels, open onto the motor court beyond. OPPOSITE: The winding stair, with stained oak treads and blackened steel balustrade, glides beneath the second-floor "lighthouse" windows.

ABOVE: The white-painted kitchen has hardware, screened cabinet panels, and fixtures all in brass. OPPOSITE: The octagonal breakfast room looking out to the living room portico and poolside bar beyond.

OPPOSITE: The library has full-height French doors and transoms. The white-painted moldings articulate the walls, which are hand finished in pink-tinted plaster. ABOVE: The octagonal primary bath with its domed ceiling. Oeil-de-boeuf windows are matched by mirrors at the interior walls. The floor is polished Paloma limestone. PAGES 192-193: The waterfront façade overlooking the pool; at the left is a loggia for outdoor living and dining, and to the right is the poolside bar.

ABOVE: The poolside bar, with pink and cream cast-stone paving, attenuated octagonal columns, decorative metal fretwork, and a standing-seam lead-coated copper roof. OPPOSITE The circular swimming pool with The Little Narrows waterway beyond.

ABOVE: The guest house, with cream stucco walls, cedar shingle roof, and Greek key stucco frieze. OPPOSITE: The guest house living room with its large bay window and green-and-white terrazzo tile floor.

SAGG POND COMPOUND

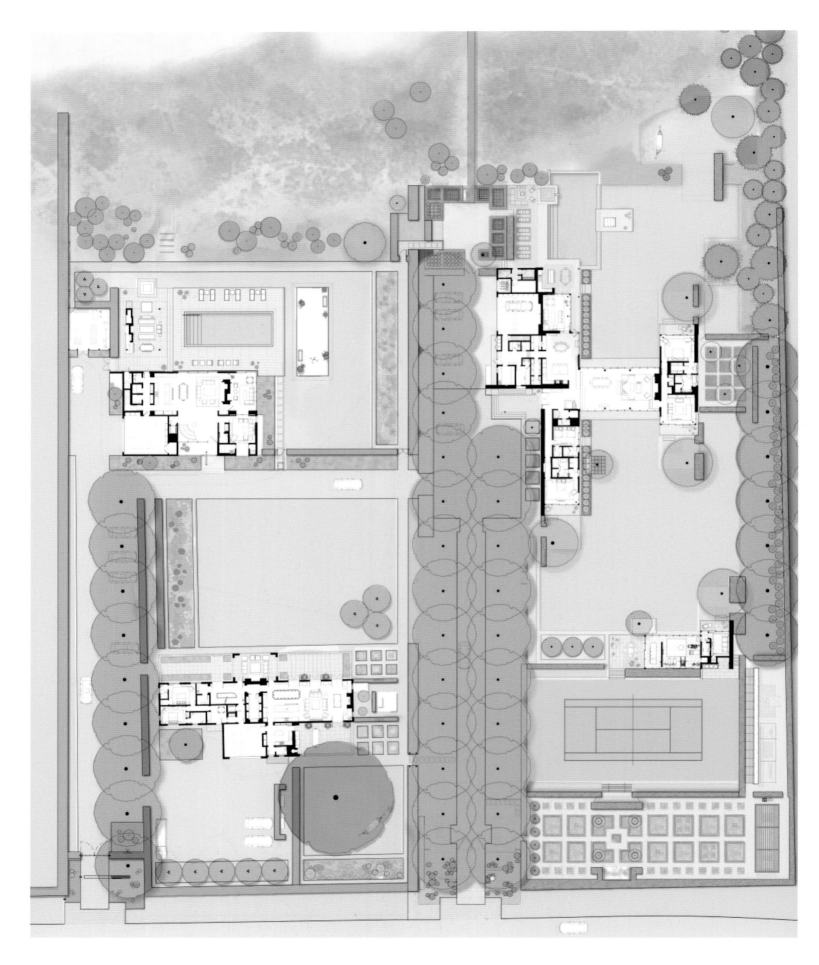

ABOVE The plan of the compound. The Main House is at the right, below which is the tennis house, tennis court, and parterre garden. At the upper left is the Pond House and at the lower left is the Barn House.

PAGES 198-199: The entry to the compound is framed by Jerusalem limestone piers and inter-planted with clipped boxwood atop a field of shore juniper groundcover. London plane trees flank the crushed-gravel drive, providing a shaded allée beyond the double gates with a view to Sagg Pond. ABOVE: A view of the Main House entry through the motor court, which is paved with granite setts. The sculptural Japanese maple punctuates the formal geometry of the clipped boxwood composition along the façade of Jerusalem limestone. PAGES 202-203: The western-facing wings of the Main House. In the foreground, a gravel court shaded by an American elm extends from the media room into the gardens surrounding the main lawn.

THIS PROJECT began when the clients came to us after seeing a house we had completed a few years earlier on the ocean in Bridgehampton, New York. The clients—three adult siblings and their mother—had purchased a waterfront property on Sagg Pond just down the street and were looking to build a modern home for themselves.

This led to a decades-long relationship, during which we designed two more houses and gardens for the family on adjacent properties. From the start, we enjoyed a wonderful collaboration with Randi Puccio of LRS Designs, who was responsible for designing and executing the interiors of all three houses.

Main House

ABOVE: Beneath a pergola, a black granite fountain flanks the approach to the mahogany and bronze front doors.
OPPOSITE: The stair's walnut treads are supported by a steel-and-bronze stringer. A mahogany rail caps a bronze balustrade.
PAGES 206-207: The dining area of the kitchen with walnut cabinetry, grey granite countertops, and limestone floors.

THIS FIRST HOME was originally meant for all four family members and thus required four bedroom suites. We looked at pinwheel floor plan and massing precedents, especially among the early projects of Mies van der Rohe and Frank Lloyd Wright.

The house is entered from the side through a porch that includes a vanishing-edge granite fountain. The main floor contains two bedroom suites, a living room, media room, kitchen, screened porch and outdoor kitchen, dining ter-

race, and a swimming pool with views over Sagg Pond. The second-floor volume contains the other two bedroom suites.

The landscape includes the driveway, with its allée of London plane trees leading to the motor court paved with granite setts. At the pond's edge is a wetlands buffer of native plantings. Broad lawns flank the living room, and the tennis house overlooks a partially sunken tennis court. Hidden behind the tennis court is an expansive vegetable and cutting garden with a dining pergola.

PAGES 208-209: The walnut-paneled main bedroom with a view east to Sagg Pond. PAGES 210-211: The swimming pool and its flanking terraces engage with the outdoor kitchen and dining wing of the house. These outdoor living areas are bordered by the restored wetland along the western edge of Sagg Pond. ABOVE: A gridded parterre of Liriope, punctuated by crape myrtles, creates a view from a ground floor bath. OPPOSITE: Behind the swimming pool is a garden with beds for herbs framed by clipped boxwood hedges. The solid limestone steps articulate the subtle changes in grade. The garden features a steel mesh sculpture by Charles Harlan. PAGES 214-215: The structure of the vegetable and cutting garden is provided by a grid of planting beds framed by clipped boxwood and divided by gravel paths. The ten-foot fence and hedge protect the garden from unwanted visitors. Fruits, vegetables, herbs, and flowers, grown without pesticides or artifical fertilizers, present a variety of colors, smells, and textures throughout the growing season.

Pond House

PAGES 216-217: The Pond House seen from the Barn House lawn. ABOVE: The white stucco and silvered mahogany front entry of the Pond House features a pivoting gate leading to the front door. OPPOSITE: The double-height entry features a semicircular steel-framed stair sheathed in plaster and white oak.

THIS HOUSE was designed as a weekend getaway for one of the three siblings. She wanted a modern house that would easily integrate indoor and outdoor living to take maximum advantage of the site's garden landscape and sweeping views of Sagg Pond. We were inspired by Samuel Marx's 1952 Tom May house in Los Angeles, where a glass-clad first floor is surmounted by an upper volume of stucco cantilevered over a swimming pool, with a flat-roofed cabana at one end.

Our design, following this precedent, consists of two stacked, offset rectangular volumes with minimal detailing. The foyer contains a curved plaster stair and opens onto the great room, beyond which is the swimming pool terrace and loggia with an outdoor living area and kitchen. The stucco-clad upper story contains the bedrooms. The interiors were done by Randi Puccio.

The subdued landscape includes a sunken pétanque court styled as a Zen garden with lawns surrounded by perennial borders and a walkway through the wetlands to the dock.

PAGES 220-221: The living and dining room looks out to the swimming pool and Sagg Pond. At the right is a fireplace with a travertine surround and hidden drop-down TV. ABOVE: Along the wall of the bleached oak-paneled study adjacent to the stair hall is a window screened by the silvered mahogany fins on the exterior. OPPOSITE: The wall of decorative tiles with its subtle circular relief forms a backdrop to the kitchen with its white glass countertops and white oak cabinetry and floors.

OPPOSITE: The primary bathroom's floor, walls, and tub deck are crafted from Italian travertine limestone. The shower and water closet are lit by a skylight. ABOVE: The primary bedroom has sweeping views across the wetlands on Sagg Pond to the dunes and the Atlantic Ocean beyond. PAGES 226-227: The view east to Sagg Pond, with the Pond House, its swimming pool, and pétanque court. PAGES 228-229: The pétanque court was inspired by *karesansui*, the dry rock gardens of Japan. Small islands of dwarf mugo pine and juniper within the steel-edged crushed-gravel surface provide strategic obstacles for the game. In the background is a colorful border with masses of Russian sage, yucca, and Artemisia.

Barn House

PAGES 230-231: The Barn House at sunset, viewed across grasses and coneflowers that bring color and texture to contrast the deep muted tones of the wood cladding. ABOVE: The shade garden just outside the great room. OPPOSITE: The double-height great room has two tiers of steel windows and doors that flood the space with light. Materials include hand-hewn oak trusses, a board-formed concrete chimney breast, and black limestone floors.

THE BARN HOUSE was designed as an entertainment pavilion for large gatherings and as a weekend and vacation home for one of the three siblings. She wanted the house to be transitional in style, more traditionally inflected than the first house but incorporating modern elements that speak directly to the other structures as part of an architecturally unified compound.

Following this directive, we developed a barnlike gabled structure, void of eaves, cornices, and other traditional detailing. The cladding is horizontal wire-brushed mahogany, referencing the mahogany cladding of the original house but stained a deep graphite grey. The roof is standing-seam zinc, and the windows and doors are blackened steel. At the center is a gabled entry porch with an outdoor fireplace and seating. The double-height great room encompasses a kitchen, dining for fourteen people, a television area, and a billiard table. Downstairs is a cinema and upstairs are a primary bedroom suite and guest accommodations. The interior design, here as in the other houses, was done by Randi Puccio.

Outside, the great room is flanked on one side by a large terrace overlooking a broad lawn that is designed for outdoor events and surrounded by extensive perennial borders. On the other side is a private terrace with an outdoor kitchen and herb garden.

ABOVE: In the powder room, a nineteenth-century European water trough serves as a wash basin.
OPPOSITE: The entry stair hall has a black limestone floor and a blackened bronze railing; the front doors are clad in charcoal-stained and wire-brushed mahogany.

ABOVE: For the wine room, we designed the waxed oak racks to accommodate bottles of various sizes as well as cases. OPPOSITE: A view through the kitchen to the pantry with its cerused oak cabinetry, black limestone floors, and walls clad in Portuguese tile with an iridescent glaze.

ABOVE: The primary bath features a countertop and tub deck in Danby marble, stained oak floors, and glazed Portuguese tile walls. OPPOSITE: The guest room with its steel window and stained oak doors. PAGES 240-241: The view from the Pond House to the Barn House over the sunken pétanque court and croquet lawn.

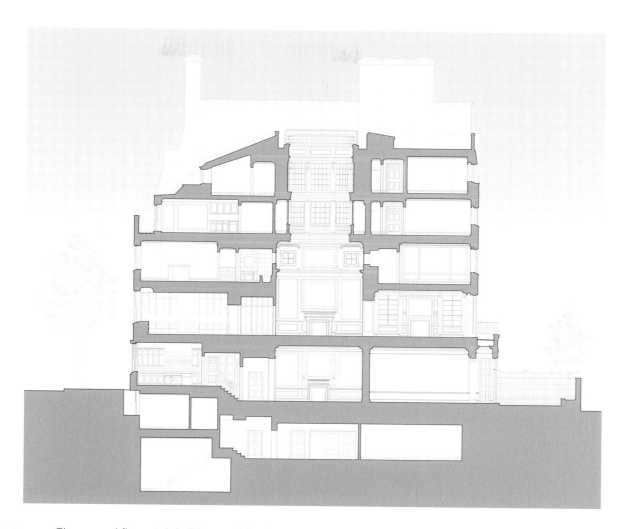

PAGES 242-243: The ground floor stair hall has strié-finished plaster paneled walls, silver travertine floors, and a fireplace. English and French antiques complement the owner's collection of art. OPPOSITE: The restored Federal-style north façade. ABOVE: A longitudinal section of the house.

THIS REMARKABLE double-wide townhouse was designed by Cross & Cross in 1922 and is a designated New York City landmark, part of a distinguished row of similarly landmarked houses.

The clients, who had lived in the townhouse for several years, came to us with a request to update their home for their growing family. This entailed a total rebuilding of the interiors, detailed in Colonial and Georgian styles to match the formality of the façade.

We recreated the first floor stair hall and replaced a formal dining room on the second floor with a modern kitchen and family room. Upstairs are a primary bedroom suite, children's bedrooms, and a new fifth story that includes an office and guest bedroom suites. The basement was expanded to accommodate a wine cellar, staff areas, and a gym. We replaced the atrium at the center of the house with a dramatic four-story space capped by an imposing skylight.

In decorating the house, we assembled a collection of new and antique pieces that respond to the Georgian architecture while also complementing the clients' antique rugs, furniture, and art. A classic palette of materials in muted tones was used throughout.

ABOVE: The guest powder room features crackled oxblood lacquer walls, a black silk ceiling, a custom mahogany and granite vanity, and an eighteenth-century Swedish mirror. OPPOSITE: The main entry hall with Georgian detailing. Inset antique mirrors are framed with gold leaf, and the owners' art hangs above an eighteenth-century Swedish commode. PAGES 248-249: The living room spans the width of the house and opens out onto the garden. The room's details are painted cast plaster, the walls are upholstered in fawn cotton velvet, and the fireplace mantel is tea-stained Italian statuary marble. The owners' antique rug sits atop the fumed white oak parquet floor inspired by Monticello, and sets the tone for the new upholstery and selection of antiques. Above the fireplace is a piece by Picasso.

PAGES 250-251: Shrouded by a canopy of trees, the garden is bordered with brick walls and scalloped painted wood lattice, festooned with English ivy. An antique mirror was added to the niche behind the "weeping rock" fountain.

ABOVE: The view of the main staircase from the stair hall. This is one of the few vestiges of the original interior. It was carefully refurbished and copied for the additional flights added above.

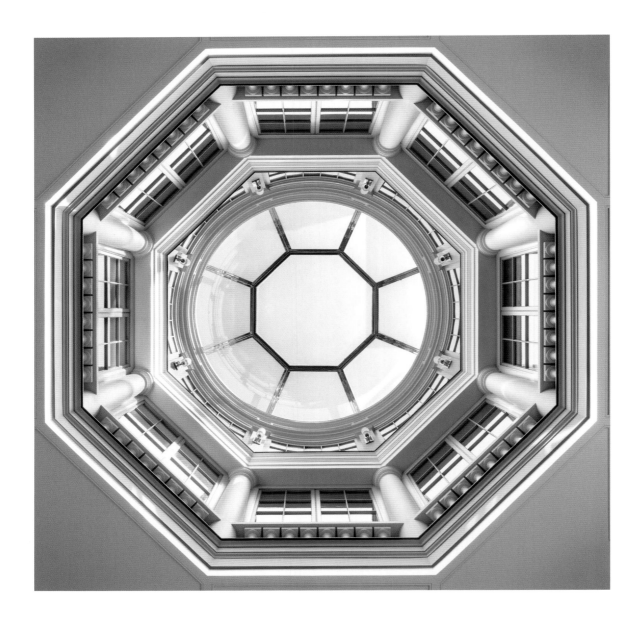

PAGE 253: Per the client's request, we created a study in solid mortise-and-tenon European walnut in the Georgian style, crafted in England and assembled on site. The furnishings were designed and upholstered to complement the owner's antique rug. Above the green marble bolection mantel is a painting by Andrew Wyeth. ABOVE: The skylight with a frame of polished stainless-steel caps the four-story atrium and lantern above the dining room. OPPOSITE: The double-height dining room occupies the base of the atrium. Strié plaster walls with woven silk inset panels are enhanced with gold leaf detailing. One-way mirrored windows above let light into third floor rooms. The walnut and gilt bronze table was designed for the room and sits atop an antique rug selected to complement the breccia marble mantel. PAGES 256-257: The materials for the modern kitchen and family room include white polyester-finished cabinets, milk glass and jet mist granite countertops, and a wall of cerused oak cabinets.

PAGES 258-259: The primary bedroom is paneled in cerused solid white English oak. The black lacquer furnishings are accompanied by a hand-woven celadon silk rug and hand-embroidered curtains. The custom curtain hardware is polished and blackened silver-plated bronze. ABOVE: The primary bath including its vanity is entirely clad in book-matched cipollino marble, with polished nickel fixtures and fittings. OPPOSITE: A guest bedroom with celadon walls and curtains along with English and Danish antiques.

ABOVE: The secondary kitchen, with pastel celadon cabinetry, Danby marble countertops, and a black limestone floor.
OPPOSITE: The service entrance stair hall is paneled in cerused white oak and furnished with an antique Portuguese console and Dutch ebony-framed mirror.

TRIBECA LOBBY AND
COURTYARD

PAGES 264-265: An aerial view of the courtyard. ABOVE: The courtyard garden is a series of interlocking pigmented cast-concrete planters containing a redbud tree and various ground cover plantings. OPPOSITE: The lobby's black-pigmented concrete dais and rectangular plinth. PAGES 268-269: The lobby's geometric wall sculpture was inspired by a 1935 white relief by the British artist Ben Nicholson.

WE WERE ASKED to design the lobby, library, and courtyard of a condominium tower in downtown Manhattan. The client's direction was very clear: the lobby would have no seating and thus would not become a gathering spot for people moving through. With this directive in mind, we envisioned minimalist spaces where bold architectural gestures would create enduring visual interest. The materials palette would be limited, as would the colors—only black, white, and grey—and the spaces would be linked by a consistent floor of pigmented concrete.

We were inspired by Donald Judd's early sculptures. The lobby's principal gesture is an ensemble of polished black concrete comprising a twelve-inch-high dais supporting a rectangular plinth. A shallow ramp is subtly integrated into the design. The lobby walls are white-framed prosceniums—two are windows to the street beyond, while the one facing you upon entry contains a white geometric sculpture inspired by a 1935 relief by the British artist Ben Nicholson, which we produced in collaboration with the artist's estate.

The minimalist black-and-white scheme continues into the library, where the walls are black-stained wood and the furniture is finished in black lacquer and leather. For the courtyard garden, we designed a geometric collage of planters in grey and black pigmented concrete containing plantings of various sizes and textures. Meant to be viewed from the apartments and corridors above, the landscape recalls Nicholson's beautiful compositions as well as the balance and order of the *karesansui* dry rock gardens of Japan.

PAGES 270-271: The library floor is pigmented concrete, the walls are black-stained wood, and the furniture is black lacquer and leather. ABOVE: The inset book display and library table with integral shelving are black lacquer. OPPOSITE: The courtyard garden plantings include compact cherry laurel, Japanese painted fern, and cushion moss. The tree is a white flowering eastern redbud.

GREENWICH VILLAGE
APARTMENT

PAGES 274-275 The dining room doubles as a cabinet of curiosities including a trove of taxidermy passed down from Brian's great uncle. The paneled walls are painted slate blue with silk paper. ABOVE : On the mantel is a drawing of the Hotel de Crillon by the architect Ange-Jacques Gabriel next to two tropical birds and a black porcelain pug. OPPOSITE: The black-lacquered, gilt and cordovan dining bureau was inspired by a Maison Jansen piece, the side chairs are Kaare Klint, and the 1920s chandelier is from a college dining hall. The herringbone floors are hand-scraped and fumed white oak.

BRIAN SAWYER'S New York City apartment is located in a historic Victorian-era edifice of red sandstone and brick from 1883. Having lost its original features over time, a new design narrative was developed inspired by the building's history and recalling the city's domestic interiors of the late nineteenth and early twentieth centuries.

The assignment provided a unique opportunity to study the architectural and design elements of the era. Windows, doors and transoms, moldings, paneling, flooring, and fireplaces were detailed to match the building's Edwardian aesthetic. Inspired by art galleries of the period, a multicolored laylight was added to frame the living room's studio skylight.

The decorating includes a mixture of custom and antique furnishings interspersed with modernist pieces complementing the historical architecture. Sawyer is an avid collector and the apartment houses many paintings, prints, drawings, fossils, sculpture, and various objets d'art that celebrate his fascination with the past.

PAGES 278-279: The living room laylight was designed to imitate those in nineteenth-century galleries. The artwork is mostly by friends, including Tom Borgese, Fernando Bengochea, Michael Hainey, and Ross Bleckner. The salvaged fireplace was found in New York.

LEFT: Above the Portoro marble mantel is a "nebula" oil painting by Tom Borgese in a Dutch-style frame together with a collection of jade Chinese congs as well as an ancient gongshi, or scholar's rock. PAGES 282-283: The primary bedroom has a series of gesso and ink drawings along with a collection of Egyptian onyx jars placed atop an original 1883 mantel.

Brian Sawyer and John Berson, New York City, 2023.

ACKNOWLEDGMENTS

IN OUR NEARLY 25 years of practice, we've had the pleasure and privilege of working with many wonderful, talented collaborators. We owe thanks to all, and the work on these pages is a testament to our shared creative endeavor.

Our sincere gratitude and appreciation to the team at Rizzoli for taking on this book and for their care and patience throughout the process: publisher Charles Miers, editors Philip Reeser and Ilaria Fusina, and production manager Alyn Evans. To book designers Mary Shanahan and Agnethe Glatved, we are deeply grateful for fashioning a seamless visual narrative from our disparate stylistic forays. Many heartfelt thanks to principal photographers Joshua McHugh and Eric Piasecki, as well as Scott Frances, Francois Dischinger, and William Waldron for their beautiful work.

Writer Mayer Rus has been our dear friend and eloquent advocate for more than 20 years. He first wrote about us in 2003 and we are honored that he embraced the task of writing the introduction as well as providing advice and support for the entire project.

We are indebted to everyone at Architectural Digest. Paige Rense and Suzanne Stephens first published our work in the pages of the magazine. Margaret Russell, with great faith and kindness, placed us on the AD100 list. Amy Astley and Alison Levasseur continue to encourage and support our enterprise to this day. Their care and confidence in us have been invaluable.

Thanks to Robert A.M. Stern and partners Roger Seifter, Paul Whalen, and Graham Wyatt, whose mentorship and training provided the professional foundation for our practice.

We are grateful to our many clients for their trust in us and the wonderful opportunities they have brought to our lives; in particular, those who generously allowed us to share their personal worlds in this book.

Our deepest thanks to our dedicated staff, present and past. The projects in this volume are a tribute to their commitment and talent. Special thanks to Karen Pelella, Alex Wilk, Tim Orlando, and Albert Yadao, whose work is featured in this book.

Lastly, Brian dedicates this book to his parents, Lynn and David Sawyer, and thanks John, his steadfast and brilliant partner. John dedicates this book to his daughters, Sasha and Natalie, whom he treasures above all else.

ARCHITECTURE

Raphael Alba
Tricia Alvez
Andrew Borek
Timothy Boyle
Maureen Brown
Kevin Browning, Senior Associate
Jonathan Bryer
Westley Burger
Anthony Campusano, Associate
Lauren Capps
Esther Cho
Lydia Chou
Elisa Cuaron, Associate
Keith Daily
Adam Dello Buono
Bradley Devendorf
Joseph Di Bella
Alane Ebner
Robert Epley, Associate
Jeremy Erdreich
Finnur Emilsson Fenger
Jonathan Ferrari
Eric Feuster, Associate
Andrea Flamenco
Christian Foster
Carmen Gonzalez
Jacob Hardin
Karl Hohlman
Tyler Horsley
Jason Iplixian
Patricia Keehn
Adam Kehr
Alex Kim
Malaika Kim, Associate
Suji Kim
Helene Kircher
Greg Koester, Studio Director
Caroline Kruis
Jennifer Lee
Munyoung Lee
Susan Link
Ricardo Lopes-Luna
Lesley Ann Malapit
Zoe Malliaros
Andre Mellone
Caroline Morgan
Mary Charlotte Osborne
Kevin O'Sullivan
Hilary Padget
Victoria Pai
Stella Papadopoulos
Thomas Papp
Karen Pelella, Senior Associate
Erik Peterson, Associate

Anthony Polito
Jennifer Pynn
Jessica Reyes
Allen Robinson, Associate
Sofia Mendes Saraiva
Kanna Sato-Chioldi
Julie Saunders
Lauren Scott
Jona Shehu
Timothy Slattery, Associate
Stephanie Smith
Cara Soh
Belinda Sosa
Fai Hung Tang
Chris Thibodeau
Andrew Thomson
Janeth Vega-Flores
William Vincent
Daniel Webre
Ashley White
Alex Wilk, Senior Associate
Albert Yadao, Associate
Jennifer Yang
Jesus Yepez
Gabriel Yi
Mahjabeen Zaheda
Marcus Ziemke

LANDSCAPE ARCHITECTURE

Adam Cesanek
Vella Chan
Yun Fan
Justin Fulweiler
Yue Guan, Associate
Toshihiko Karato
Payal Mody
Alex Ochoa
Tim Orlando, Senior Associate
Yirui Pan
Sara Peschel
Alex Pisha
Sarah Porter
Catharine Rha
David Seiter
Adrian Smith
Susan Wisniewski
Andi Yang

INTERIOR DESIGN

Aman Ahluwalia
Chris Dawson, Director
Rogelio Garcia, Director
Joshua Greene, Director
Katrina Hernandez

Iris Kim
Nicole LaPeruta
Matt McKay, Director
Javier Ortega
Jose Luis Sobrino, Director
Katie Stoltman
Courtney Stubbs Hunter

VISUALIZATION

Dante Baldassin
Marisol Reed
Whitney Shanks
Tian Yao
Duo Zhang

ADMINISTRATION

Ayelet Arbuckle
Amelia Black
Rebecca Ferris
Victoria Florio
Halley Freger
Lisa Gross
Rosemary Hill
Francis Holstrom
Angie Kwak
Kelly Lilly
Jennifer Liseo
Marianne Miskiewicz
Emily Sartor
Louis Schefano
Matthew Thomas

PROJECT CREDITS

SOUTHAMPTON MODERN
Architect and Landscape Architect:
Sawyer | Berson; Project Managers Alex Wilk and
William Vincent (architecture), Toshi Karato
(landscape architecture)
General Contractor: Koral Bros. Inc.
Landscape Contractor: Landscape Details, Inc.
Interior Designer: Stephen Sills Associates

EAST END COMPOUND
Architect, Landscape Architect and Interior Designer:
Sawyer | Berson; Project Managers
Erik Peterson (architecture), Sarah Porter and
Tim Orlando (landscape architecture), Jose Luis
Sobrino (interior design)
General Contractor: Bulgin & Associates Inc.
Landscape Contractor: Whitmores Inc.

WAINSCOTT BEACH HOUSE
Architect and Landscape Architect:
Sawyer | Berson; Project Managers Malaika Kim
(architecture), David Seiter (landscape architecture)
General Contractor: John Hummel and Associates
Landscape Contractor: Whitmores Inc.
Interior Designer: Denise Kuriger Design, LTD.

MID-CENTURY MODERN
Architect and Landscape Architect:
Sawyer | Berson; Project Managers John Berson
and Brian Sawyer (architecture), Sarah Porter
(landscape architecture)
General Contractor: Sandy Allan Builders
Landscape Contractor: Verderber's Landscape
Nursery Inc.

COLONIAL REVIVAL
Architect, Landscape Architect and Interior Designer:
Sawyer | Berson; Project Managers Gregory Koester
and Elisa Cuaron (architecture), Tim Orlando (landscape
architecture), Josh Greene (interior design)
General Contractor: Wright & Company
Construction, Inc.
Landscape Contractor: Landscape Details, Inc.

BRIDGEHAMPTON HOUSE
Architect and Landscape Architect:
Sawyer | Berson; Project Managers Karen Pelella
(architecture), Toshi Karato (landscape architecture)
General Contractor: John Hummel and Associates
Landscape Contractor: Summerhill Landscapes, Inc.
Interior Designer: Damon Liss Design

GEORGICA POND HOUSE
Architect and Landscape Architect:
Sawyer | Berson; Project Managers

Stella Papadopoulos (architecture), Tim Orlando
(landscape architecture)
General Contractor: Wright & Company
Construction, Inc.
Landscape Contractor: Whitmores Inc.
Interior Designer: S.R. Gambrel, Inc.

SOUTHAMPTON CONTEMPORARY
Architect and Landscape Architect:
Sawyer | Berson; Project Managers John Berson and
Stella Papadopoulos (architecture), Sarah Porter
(landscape architecture)
General Contractor: Bulgin & Associates Inc.
Landscape Architect: Reed Hilderbrand LLC,
Eric Kramer, Project Manager
Landscape Contractor: Whitmores Inc.
Interior Designers: Bonetti/Kozerski Architecture D.P.C;
Kelly Behun Studio

NORTH SEA MINIMAL
Architect and Landscape Architect:
Sawyer | Berson; Project Managers Alex Wilk
(architecture), Toshi Karato (landscape architecture)
General Contractor: BK Kuck Construction
Landscape Contractor: Superior Landscaping
Solutions, Inc.
Interior Designer: Richard Shemtov / Dune

SAG HARBOR FEDERAL
Architect and Landscape Architect:
Sawyer | Berson; Project Managers Albert Yadao
(architecture), Toshi Karato (landscape architecture)
General Contractor: Bulgin & Associates Inc.
Landscape Contractor: Landscape Details, Inc.
Interior Designer: Groves & Co., Pamela Meech,
Project Manager

NOYACK REGENCY
Architect and Landscape Architect:
Sawyer | Berson; Project Managers Karen Pelella,
Susan Link and Jacob Hardin (architecture),
Toshi Karato (landscape architecture)
General Contractor: Frank Cafone Construction, Inc.
Landscape Contractor: Landscape Details, Inc.
Interior Designer: Daniel Romualdez Architects

SAGG POND COMPOUND MAIN HOUSE
Architect and Landscape Architect:
Sawyer | Berson; Project Managers Keith Daily and
Timothy Boyle (architecture), Tim Orlando
(landscape architecture)
General Contractor: Wright & Company
Construction, Inc.
Landscape Contractor: Whitmores Inc.
Interior Designer: Randi Puccio, LRS Designs

SAGG POND COMPOUND POND HOUSE
Architect and Landscape Architect:
Sawyer | Berson; Project Managers Jeremy Erdreich
and Jacob Hardin (architecture), Tim Orlando
(landscape architecture)
Landscape Contractor: Whitmores Inc.
Interior Designer: Randi Puccio, LRS Designs

SAGG POND COMPOUND BARN HOUSE
Architect and Landscape Architect:
Sawyer | Berson; Project Managers Jeremy Erdreich,
Jacob Hardin and Elisa Cuaron (architecture),
Tim Orlando (landscape architecture)
General Contractor: John Hummel and Associates
Landscape Contractor: Whitmores Inc.
Interior Designer: Randi Puccio, LRS Designs

MANHATTAN TOWNHOUSE
Architect and Interior Designer: Sawyer | Berson;
Project Managers Karen Pelella (architecture),
Jose Luis Sobrino (interior design)
General Contractor: SMI Construction Management Inc.

TRIBECA LOBBY AND COURTYARD
Architect, Landscape Architect and Interior Designer:
Sawyer | Berson; Project Managers
Elisa Cuaron (architecture), Tim Orlando (landscape
architecture), Matt McKay (interior design)
General Contractor: Foundations Group, Inc.
Plantings Contractor: Artisan Gardens, LLC

GREENWICH VILLAGE APARTMENT
Architect and Interior Designer: Sawyer | Berson;
Project Managers Erik Peterson (architecture),
Jose Luis Sobrino (interior design)
General Contractor: SilverLining Inc.

Cover, endpapers and **pages 2–4** by Joshua McHugh

Southampton Modern: Joshua McHugh

East End Compound: Joshua McHugh

Wainscott Beach House: Eric Piasecki

Mid-Century Modern: Francois Dischinger
pages 76, 77, 78–79, 81, 82–83, 84–85;
Michael Moran/OTTO p. 80; Eric Piasecki pages 74–75

Colonial Revival: Joshua McHugh
pages 86–87, 89, 90, 96, 100–101, 102, 103, 104–105;
Eric Piasecki pages 91, 92–93, 94–95, 97, 98, 99

Bridgehampton House: Joshua McHugh

Georgica Pond House: Eric Piasecki

Southampton Contemporary: William Waldron

North Sea Minimal: Joshua McHugh

Sag Harbor Federal: Joshua McHugh

Noyack Regency: Joshua McHugh

Sagg Pond Compound Main House: Joshua McHugh,
pages 201, 202–203, 204,
206–207, 208–209, 210–211, 212, 213, 214–215;
Eric Piasecki page 205
Sagg Pond Compound Pond House: Joshua McHugh
Sagg Pond Compound Barn House: Joshua McHugh

Manhattan Townhouse: Scott Frances/OTTO,
pages 242–243, 244, 246, 247, 248–249, 250–251,
252, 254, 255, 258–259, 260, 261;
Eric Piasecki, pages 253, 256–257, 262, 263

Tribeca Lobby and Courtyard: Alexander Severin

Greenwich Village Apartment: Joshua McHugh,
pages 274–275, 277, 278–279, 280–281, 282–283;
Roger Davies/OTTO, page 276

Portrait on page 284 by John Huba

First published in the United States of America in 2023 by
Rizzoli International Publications, Inc.
300 Park Avenue South
New York, New York 10010
www.rizzoliusa.com

Publisher: Charles Miers
Editors: Philip Reeser and Ilaria Fusina
Production manager: Alyn Evans
Design coordinator: Olivia Russin
Proofreader: Claudia Bauer
Managing editor: Lynn Scrabis

Design by Mary Shanahan and Agnethe Glatved
Editorial production by Vincent Spina

ISBN: 978-0-8478-6372-3
Library of Congress Control Number: 2023931015
2023 2024 2025 2026 / 10 9 8 7 6 5 4 3 2 1
Printed in Hong Kong